REFERENCE

MERCY WARD

D1390209

Mercy Ward

IAN McDONALD

PETERLOO POETS

WITHDRAWN

SCOTTISH POETRY LIBRARY
Tweeddale Court 14 High Street
Edinburgh EH1 1TE
Tel: 031-557 2876

Ian McDonald (D)

First published in 1988
by Peterloo Poets
2 Kelly Gardens, Calstock, Cornwall PL18 9SA

© 1988 by Ian McDonald

All rights reserved. No part of this publication may be
reproduced, stores in a retrieval system, or transmitted, in any
form or by any means, electronic, mechanical, photocopying,
recording or otherwise without the prior permission in writing of
the publisher.

ISBN 0 905291 95 6

Printed in Great Britain by
Latimer Trend & Company, Plymouth

8149
(21.4.90)
C

ACKNOWLEDGEMENTS

Some of these poems first appeared in *Kyk-over-al* and *Jamaica Review*.

"I wish to thank Stewart Brown for his enthusiasm and encouragement when I showed him these poems and for his help in getting them published. They would be languishing in a bottom drawer were it not for him. I would like also to thank Bridget Evelyn for all her help in typing the poems."—Ian McDonald.

WITH THE ASSISTANCE OF

SOUTH WEST ARTS

To my wife, Mary,
and in memory of
my grandmother, Hilda McDonald

Contents

Life/Death

Sudden,
Quick as light:
Skin shine,
Then
Bone white.

Just Johnny On His Chart

Johnny on his chart,
Simply Johnny,
Helplessly small.
His large head slips sideways,
A stick arm hangs listless out the cot
Like a last gesture for help.
Eyes look at you:
Blue-black in the corners,
Flickering, searching, ending.
Don't look at the eyes.
I feel like shouting out
Hold him quick!
He slips on the world like grease,
Soon fall off.

Nurse Guyadeen And The Preacher

Best nurse in here was Sati Guyadeen
Bright, loving, strict, humorous and clean.
Dealt briskly with every single chore
Yet strove beyond "Accept, endure."
Sati Guyadeen, fresh morning breeze,
Stepping in on edge of dance,
You made a difference in this place.
Who claims even half-perfection?
Hope and bravery in every glance
You nudged life in the right direction.

Big feud broke out once in here:
It livened up the Ward a while.
They brought in Herman Forrester
A pavement-preacher all his life.
He had his pitch in Water Street:
Up and down the pave all day,
"Save your soul: Repent, repent!
The world it end tonight at eight.
Repent, repent! It not too late!"
Every Friday eleven o'clock
He took his stand by Royal Bank:
"Money is the root of all evil,
It eat out your soul like biscuit-weevil!"
And Wednesday by J. P. Santos store
He lectured on Mosaic law.

In here he didn't stop for breath
All day you heard his preacher-mouth:
"Repent your sins before you die!"
If you were God's children, then all right:
He pointed straight up in the sky.
But when he said where sinners go
He pointed dramatically low
Implying that those he saw around
Would taste hell-fire underground.
In all the Ward distress began:
They frighten of this preacher man.

11

Who with, say, a month to go
Likes to be condemned below?

Nurse Guyadeen, brisk and firm,
Decide herself to handle him.
"People can't have peace in here?
Hush up, or water pour on you!"
(She would have poured a drop or two).
The big feud start up straight away:
Preacher-man forget to preach,
He have a new thing now to do:
Bad-talking Guyaden black and blue.
"Parrot-monkey, La Penitence rat,
Guyadeen more ugly than that!"
He spends his hours thinking hard
And looking happy when he could shout
"Someone smell like pit-latrine
It must have to be Nurse Guyadeen!"
And Guyadeen giving as good as got
Lip match lip, hot for hot
And when she think he gets too fas'
She jam an enema up his arse.
The quarrel kept the whole Ward bright:
Who win today was the talk tonight.
For a good ten days they had it out
Row for row, shout for shout,
But I noticed how she took her cue:
He began to weaken, she weakened too.
The last few days it didn't count
His mind wandered North and South
Sweet Jesus walked in Stabroek Market
And hóney rained on Zion's Mount.
"Good riddance!" claimed nurse Guyadeen
When she came to hear he died at noon;
Set straight about her many tasks,
Brought clean sheets, plumped up the pillows.
The empty bed was filled by six,
The new chart written up and fixed.
She made sure the night-lamps all were lit
And then she cried a little bit.

Belle Of The Ball

"Why is she in rags?"
Silk dress, but in shreds now
Flowered, faded, aged, and filthy.
It was made for bigger breasts
And plumper hips and sweeter thighs:
Eighty pounds at least are missing.
A heap of bones in this strange silk.
"She wanted to wear it:
She is dying, why not let her?"
What dance does she remember,
What dancing days,
When that nice dress once made her
Belle of the Ball?

Walking In The Stars

Last words are not remarkable as a rule.
They drift away, have nothing much to say,
Murmurs hardly loud enough to catch the ear:
"Please for some water", "I so cold in here".
Not more nor less than this or that.
Dying is a puzzled, incoherent act.
But this one! He described his desert days,
Rose-coloured forts and old battalion pals.
"Servant of the Crown", one of the old school,
He served the King in post-war Palestine.

One still, clear night in Galilee
The stars dripped silver in a midnight sea.
He and his platoon went wading out
Far from shore so that they could shout
Loud among the stars and be heard by God.
He ends before he ends the story:
A sentence cut in half is his last word.
His exultant voice clamours to be heard:
"I, walking in the stars, in great glory ... "

Axed Man

"Bad-bad case of sugar:
They had to cut him down".
The old man sits upright, rigid,
Spine straight against heaped pillows.
He grips the bedclothes on both sides.
Big-torsoed, bull-necked, muscled man
Wears faded-red, short pyjama pants
Just folding over both new bandaged stumps.
No toes, no feet, no shins, no legs
No knees to kneel on any longer
To pray to God for mercy, rest.
Yesterday they "cut him down" again
But still an obscure stink prevails.

Matron knows his story: strong once,
A timber man, big as the trees he killed.
He lived in forests and towered over men,
A rollicking and famous working man:
Ten times won at Mashramani time
Who could chop a great tree down the fastest.
He logged purple-heart and teak and silverballi:
Trees falling give a sense of exultation.
Look at his stumps now!
The axe in the end
Missed horribly.

Fire In The Ward

Young, new nurse, serious in her job:
White uniform, white as roses,
Brushed lustrous hair, brownskin shining.
She seems a banked immortal fire,
Warm beauty, such glow of life.

She passed between the beds
Full of vigour, dance, and glory.
As she passes, they sink lower down
They seem ashamed, avoid her eyes.
She blazes: they shrink far away.
You think, they should die quicker
Get out of the way of health and beauty.
What is the use of living any more,
Hips will never sway like that again?
She is burning this place down,
They will all be lost.

Motherly old dump, old Matron,
With your greyness, limp and sighs,
Better you walk this ward.

Granny Isaacs Versus Death

Granny Isaacs, from the time she came,
Fought death like a tiger.
She looked ready to go from day one:
Frail as a stick in the sun,
Tissue paper for her skin,
Old, toothless mouth caved in,
Hair lank and loose and ivory.
So thin, bones showed:
The next thing would be skeleton.

But she battled for life
And would not give in.
She hurried to take her food,
Sat up when and where she could,
Was eager to keep presentable,
And tried conversing quite a bit.
She would not just go.

And, most of all,
She made it clear,
She placed her faith
In God's arrangements
And that beyond
This fierce encounter
Other ceremonies are planned.

It could be said
Death came out top.
Who can be sure?
She made me think
Now she has gone
We'll have to wait
A little more
To see who won.

Time Piece

There is no clock in here:
The tick-tock of what time left
Is lost told too sad a doom.
And it disturbed the restless night
To hear the loud knock-knocking:
It was like drip-drop, drip-drop
Blood falling to the floor
And no one ever coming.
So they took it out.

It wouldn't matter now,
They could bring back a clock.
These days
Clocks are different:
Soft, no noise.
They do not beat
Like hearts
That stop.

The Last Classroom Of Hubertus Jones

Hubertus Jones was teacher to the bone:
Fifty years in schools in Golden Grove.
His wit unvarying as the texts he taught:
Mark him down five in scale ten to nought.
Term after term infinitely unwound
Plain and strict and dull and sound.
Taught unchanging what he could teach,
The generations soared beyond his reach.
Cord-thin, very neat, and spare
His routines recurring, his rules austere,
He made no money, so he ended here.

People lonely, sick, and old
Have strange dreams in Mercy Ward:
When they "go off" no fuss is made,
They are soothed or chided, then tucked back in.
So Schoolmaster Jones pursued his career,
Taught a full class and set them homework.
Once a week he had Matron fired
For failing to do what he required
And confirmed in writing to Central Board
All that was wrong in Mercy Ward.

What eases the heart should never be grudged:
When anyone departed his last classroom
Hubertus Jones called for paper and pen
And it was seriously brought for him to compose
A concise and lucid term's review
Of conduct, aptitude, and future ambitions
For possible use by the powers that be.
He carefully handed them in on completion
And Matron would promise to deliver them safe.
Meticulous in all he ever did
He kept file copies for easy referral.

When Hubertus Jones departed in turn
I had a look at his filed returns.
Everyone was given precisely his due
But I noticed something shining through:

In the very worst cases of condemnation
He always added a last recommendation:
"Whatever his misdemeanours here on earth
He should be given a chance to prove his worth".

Scrappy little man, Hubertus Jones:
God spare us all, and rest his bones.

Not Here

Somewhere
A bird sings.
Sound of ping-pong balls
Batted to and fro,
Kitchen-clatterings,
A shooing of dogs.
Wind-murmurs
In green trees.
Laughter-spiced talk
Somewhere,
Not here.

Screaming Girl

It is no use to pretend otherwise:
This is not a pleasant, airy place.
They try their best with pots of flowers,
Prints of sunny seas and bright savannas,
But it would be foolish to expect good cheer.
In fact, it very much surprises one,
With so much pain and sickness all about,
How quiet it is always: a few low sounds, creaking of a bed.

Alarming and mysterious, then, suddenly to hear
A girl screaming as if her life gave out,
Screaming and screaming as they hold her arms:
It must be worse than pain that visits her!
She screams, it is hard to pity or excuse it:
The thought of death is worse than death itself
And she is young, you think: so much to lose.
It is not quite so simple, as you soon discover.
For hygiene's sake, and discipline, and work routine
They can't allow this girl's hair shining to her thighs
And she disturbs the whole room with her agony.
They snip it off in lustrous curls piling on the floor
And the girl screams, more and more and more.

There is, I must suppose, a deeper wound to bear
Than any mortal injury that doctors diagnose
But what it is in this girl's case
I find, amid the screaming, I do not know or care.

Royal Visit

Once Mercy Ward was heaped with flowers.
A serious princess from the British Isles
Asked what more duty she could do
To fill a Sunday morning she had spare.
They really spruced the place up then:
Cleaners scrubbed the floor with non-carbolic soap,
Swept roach wings, mouse shit, all away,
Air freshener used to help the winds of May.
Mercy Ward was clean as heaven.

And everywhere it blazed with flowers.
The Parks Commission sent their gardeners.
Truckloads of greenery and flowers came:
Great, lovely clumps of flaming bougainvillea,
Roses in profusion and Barbados Pride,
Blue plumbago and sweet jump-up-and-kiss,
Vases lent and filled with fragrant plants,
Exotic orchids pale in beds of fern,
Blood-red hibiscus and flowers of the sun.
(Would all their funerals fetch half so much?).

Only old Mangru, not known for being difficult,
Spoiled the great occasion somewhat.
When she stopped and asked him very nicely how he was
He sucked his few teeth quite hard and long:
For all the sour stares from Matron at the back
He simply would not smile or say a single word.
Even worse than that, old-stager Mangru,
When she was three beds further on,
Amidst the healthy dignitaries, all those lovely blooms,
Gave forth the loudest fart you ever, ever heard.

Discharged

They cannot keep you in this place
If you are sure you do not want to stay.
You can discharge yourself at any time:
You have that option, it is your privilege.
Naturally they try to persuade you differently.
Mostly it is possible to ease the patient back
But sometimes a little vigour must be used:
The tough attendants use a slap or two
To make a man see sense, and only for his sake.

But one night, dismal with a rainy moon,
The young man in row 6, bed 22,
Solitary, silent, making no fuss at all,
Broke a hidden drinking glass
And under the covering sheets pulled right up
Cut both his wrists, deeply, surely,
One by one carefully, firmly,
And discharged himself.
They came running in the morning
But not even the tough ones
Could coax him back.

The Last Good Shout

To people clinging on to life
It takes not much to satisfy;
It's also not fully understood
In what extremity life still seems good.
Things are measured differently:
Simple gifts are jamboree.
Please God, stretch the hours out:
Might perhaps be one last good shout!

Diwali festival one year
A big rice farmer sent piles of fruit:
Ripe mango, pine, and golden apple.
Who too sick to eat enjoy to look:
"We just feel good we get it free".
The same day be coincidence
Rampaging children visited.
Throwing, catching, red balloons
They soon escape their mother's care.
"Man, don't concern, let them make noise".
Race round laughing, bumping into beds,
Playing catcher and bounce-balloon.
A good thing matron isn't here:
A playground buzz hangs wildly in the air.
Pray God this day not end too soon!

Fuss-pot

The old woman never stopped complaining:
It seemed her sign of life, her signature.
The food was bad or salt or made her sick,
Water had the bitter taste of aloes in her mouth,
Bed was hard or full of lumps or flea-infested,
The light was bad, mosquitoes stung her toes,
The place was hot or cold, whichever was most trouble,
And she never got the right amount of good attention.
And whenever the children visited, she let them have her tongue.

She deserved the suck-teeth she all the time received.
Strange, then, at the end, when agony came on,
She was calm and quiet as the day is long.
Lay back and never made a single petty call
And seemed to try and find a deepening peace within.
And when the children came you noted, with surprise,
How close they clung to her with many signs of love.

Who can delve into all the years gone by?
All one can tell is in behaviour now.
She takes on strength and certainty and love,
She summons seriousness in place of spite.
Death for her is drama worth her while
Too big, it seems, to make a fuss about.

The Master

The old man carries on so:
He has no bravery.
But we don't know
How hard he tried
Keep the cries inside
Then let go.

Pain won't go
With screaming:
Pain feeds on screams.
Praying's no good:
Please go,
Please let it go!
Drugs work a while,
Lock the pain away.
It's still there,
Waiting.
Show kindness, love:
Abashed, pain backs away.
Not for long:
It comes back again,
The hard master
That sings no song.
Pain teases:
It'll let go
For a whole hour.
That's worse:
It keeps its power.

One thing though.
Have patience,
It will go.
Old man
Wait, wait.
At last
It will go.

Candle-light

No beauty
Is here
It is stark.
But one night
Light failed
Over half the town;
The old generator
Took its time to start.
In that instant
Candle-flies in season,
Brightening and fading,
Were hundreds in the room
As if girls
Had flung them
At a wedding.

That once,
Such beauty
In this sad place,
The glimmering
Of candle-flies.

Night Fear

"Fast-Finish" Kowlessar, famous cyclist,
And, later, rum-shop raconteur,
Ended up here when his good wife died,
Stricken and trembling like water in a wind.
Sons found good reasons not to keep him
But sent of course the fruit and cigarettes he needed
For which he thanked them when they visited
Which was twice a month unless otherwise engaged.

The darkness he hated the most I've ever seen,
As if the sun went out for him alone:
He cried with fear and loneliness at night,
This brave man who once won famous races.
He could not bear the coming on of night.
The rose of evening, and his fear would start,
And never until morning would it depart.

Night's the worst time, that's sure,
People die much more.
More people do not die,
Death is just much more.

One nurse kept him company for a while at night
Listening to stories of his young days and his sons
Wide-opening her eyes: she had the art
To show her fascination for all he said.
I think she kept the dark from closing round his heart.
But she was reprimanded, as she was bound to be,
For neglecting other chores for "Fast Finish" Kowlessar:
The night she suddenly was not there
For those who saw it, it was hard to bear.

There's one good thing about what we really hate:
The end of it is sweet beyond compare.
They could have told him, or he should have known,
The longest night of all contains no fear.

Chasing Flies

The day is over in the Ward.
The dark time gathers in my room.
In and out of cloudy caverns
A silver, chill moon falls and floats.
Rain spots the window where I sit.

Too much to do today:
The blur and fade of routine work.
The mind that holds a universe
Will keep a single memory fresh.

In noon-time's sultry heat
A beaten old man falls asleep:
Snoring toothless mouth agape
Yawning in a ravaged face.
Not much there to talk about.
With tender art that will not last
A young nurse coming up to him
Bends down so carefully concerned,
Gently shoos some flies away,
Secures the boon of sleep for him
And steps away with quiet grace.

The silver moon streams where I sit
Three years at least have passed away
And still I sometimes think of it.

Test Match

When cricket is playing
This place has a special mood.
Naturally, in the town there's little else.
For miles and miles and miles around
Attention centres on the Test Match ground:
Stands besieged from early morning;
Transistored cyclists weave one-handed,
Risking crashes every wicket down.
Heroic men are just down there
And the greatest heroes are our own.
Latest score is all that counts,
There is a feel of fair-ground in the air.

It catches on in Mercy Ward,
The excitement rises in the days before,
The desperate centring on self departs.
The subject concentrated on is changed,
The endless question unexpressed:
How much time have I got left?
Now other questions supervene:
The boys in trouble or the boys on top?
Their minds, diverted and released,
Fly out to where the cricket plays.
For a little while at least
Those broken on the wheel of life
Feel at their throats a different knife.

Stealing Buxton Spice

What has made the veterans so upset:
Even the garrulous are silent and faraway?
Old Farnum shakes his head and mumbles something odd.
Shading the Ward veranda, in the yard outside,
Three tall old mango trees are full of fruit:
Rosy Buxton Spice are hanging sweet and low.
Wasps buzz and sip where bats have sucked the holes.
A lovely smell of ripeness fills the noon-time Ward.
"Touch them by the stem, they fall down in you' hand".
Boys pelt down the fruit, or climb up the trees and steal:
They do it laughing now, so did they long ago,
As Farnum, who won't go out again, and six other old men know

Monster

Black eyes
Without tears.
Terrible seeing a child
That will not cry.
A monster's eyes:
The giant worm of hunger
Swells her belly.
It lies curled there,
It has wound itself upwards
And stares out the sockets
Of her emptied eyes.

The Dwarf Dogs Of Montserrat

Jumpy on twin leashes
Panting pink tongues
Gold-speckled eyes
Scarlet-collared
Silver-tagged like gifts
Miniature and manicured:
A fine lady brings them,
Luxury-lap things.
She is sleek too.

What are they doing,
Dogs are not allowed?
This fine lady is allowed
And of course her pets.
How in this place?
You see that old woman
Crumpled in a corner bed,
Ulcers on her cheek?
The fine lady sleek as silk
Comes from Montserrat:
A mansion by the sea
Terraced with sea-grapes.
She's purchased beauty.
Two different lives ago
This old auntie minded her.

Favours are bestowed now,
New clothes and drugs.
Old woman nods and nods and nods.
The little dogs jump and yap,
Pink tongues lick her oozing cheek.
The fine lady cries.
Old auntie smiles and nods
She puts up a hand again
Shoo, shoo, dry the tears
She dried a thousand times
Time gone like forty years.

Art Exhibits

A most joyous thing in the Ward
Was once when an old lady was admitted
She brought pictures coloured by small children
And stuck them up on the wall above her bed:
Bright cartoons of green dogs and red cats
And blazing suns in cloudless skies
And perfect blue seas with white birds flying.

The last one she pinned up glowed superbly:
Grandma, no doubt, in necklaces and purple gown
Sitting in a golden chair, smiling all around.
When she went the pictures stayed a few days
Then began to fall off and were swept away.
I remember feeling sad, no one ever came for them.

White Grip

At first you couldn't see her beauty:
This young girl was too-too thin,
Bones were too near the skin:
Where could the blood find room to move?
No soft bosom, just nipples on a chest.
Look hard again, you see it soon:
No beauty ever matched hers in this room.

Oh, it is sad, sad to tell her story;
She did not expect to be here for long.
A man who went away has now come back:
They are matched, she will go with him.
The day she cannot wait for comes along,
She sits for hours combing out her hair.

He walks in and you know: nothing for her there.
He sits, her eyes fasten on his face;
His lips make up a smile, he scorns this place.
Eyes slip and slide from early on:
Five minutes, he turns to check a noise,
Ten, the first look at his golden Seiko watch.
Meanwhile she hungers, devours all of him.
His well-fed frame is squirming all about:
He's embarrassed, how quick he can get out?
Half an hour, it's his time to go, not hers:
Her lustrous eyes cannot, cannot believe it.
It's a simple thing: he made it, she has not.
He quite roughly puts aside her hand,
She grasps his arm most desperately.
No good asking how it ended
With any hope that all went well:
He went away, she died one day.

Some things once glimpsed remain mind-set:
Moon blaze on an Essequibo shore;
Hawks riding high above this waiting place;
How once a boy looked at Orion's Belt;
An old man crying in the Silver Chapel.
White grip on his arm I can't forget,
Anyway not yet, not yet.

Dark Angel

A bird flew in,
Quite big, taloned,
Perhaps it was a hawk.
It grew desperate:
Flew against shut windows,
Battered against rafters,
Begun to leave droppings.

Much excitement,
Great fluttering of wings.
Somebody screamed out:
"Out, out, get it out!"
Full of fear and hate.
The dark angel.

Stone Fish

Abel Washington is eighty-four:
He's the oldest one in here;
Life has finished with him completely.
His mouth dribbles open all day long,
Eyes have clouded the colour of the sea.
The only time he lifts his head a little:
When ice-cream comes for him to suck.
Hard to find his story when I checked:
He has disappeared before his death.
Booker Wharfinger for fifty years
In the old days when sugar sailed in sacks.
No family left at all, all dead or gone away.
Lives condensed like this is history.

Two things alone stick out for me.
He made a famous river swim
Across the Essequibo mouth and back;
And he was known as "Stone Fish" in the town;
It's a mystery: no one now knows why.
I try to ask him, but he makes no reply,
Then take his hand and sit by him
And talk about his Essequibo swim.
A sudden thing, his hand no longer slack
His eyes come level, his head unsags
For a second, for the briefest shiver.
What happened? What came back?
Is nothing lost, did he feel the river?

Getting Well

You can always tell the time for sure
When patients who are getting well
Will soon get up and leave the others here:
They do not have that one-way-only-stare.
They seem to see the flowers in the jar.
They do not make a boast of getting well:
"The kindness of the ward", it's called.

But outside you can see amazing scenes.
One time a man ran in the glorious sun
And climbed a green tree standing in the yard.
To the very top he climbed, rocking in the wind,
And turned his face up to the burst of sun,
Frolicked on a swaying branch, and scrambled down
"I'm not mad"! he cried,
And swung his mother round and round.

Amerindian

I suppose you'd say with truth
No one here looks all that "right".
But they settle themselves down.
He was all wrong from start to finish;
He squatted in his bed half the time
Paddling a strange bateau.

All his life he knew forests,
Forests and the great rivers.
Why bring him in town to die?
His soul is damned that way.
Tribal over-arching heaven
Replaced by rag of sky.

He should have been with brothers,
He should have died with jaguars and stars
And a wind rising in the trees.
A last wood-fire comforting
The coming on of cold.

Dream for him a savage vision:
A multitude of years will pass
When buildings in this upstart town
Again are lost in sea-drowned grass.
The forest will stay,
Nothing he loved gone down.

Ward Weather

The right day to die on:
A grey sky leaking rain,
Colour washed out of everything.
Whole week it's like this,
Trees groaning in the sea-wind,
Mornings sad after black nights.
Can't blame people dying today!

Last week it was different:
Humming-bird sort of weather.
Sun flaming in the sky,
Rose-smell, hot grass, and ripening pomegranates,
At night stars crackling like sparks from a fire.
In here people died then too!

Draw no conclusions from the outside weather.
Rain or bright shining sun
Ward weather is Ward weather.
I recall the sorrow of all graves
And what the old men say:
What a day to die on
Is any day!

SCOTTISH POETRY LIBRARY
Tweeddale Court 14 High Street
Edinburgh EH1 1TE
Tel: 031-557 2876

A Row About The Moon

Regular as religion, every month,
There is a row about the moon.

When the full moon comes to flower
It floods the earth with silver colour.
A basin of white water spills and froths
And slops over all the town.
A bright pallor spreads in dark corridors.

Some in Mercy Ward complain:
They hate and fear the great white ghost
That makes them think of Jumbie-birds.
They want the tall blinds pulled across:
Keep out the coffin-colour, these ones say,
Keep out the leper-shine,
This fungus-staining of our skin.

Some want the moon let in:
They like the pallid beauty everywhere,
The waxen light of lilies that it throws.
Throw the windows wide and let her in,
The grey fox of the night, our pet,
We may not see again, so sleek, so silvery,
Let her in!

Caged

The stroke stuns him into just a stare:
Mouth screams without a scream being there.
Neck muscles tighten, throat-apple thrums.
Plucks with fingers at his lips and tongue
To rip out songs or words or anything,
He strains and sweats to say a single word.
Paradise would be to let out half a cry:
Nothing comes; his eyes rage.
Think of birds that can no longer fly:
His skull is like a bolted cage,
No opening anywhere.
The slightest motion, a shivering in the cheek
Like wings in flutter before flight.
No further movement comes:
Inside there alone, alone, alone, alone,
Wings nailed right through to bone.

Sweet Pepper Sunday

Hook-nosed Amoroso,
Eyes blazing,
Spade beard bristling white,
Demanded the right
To better food.
Slop and sausages
Were not his fare,
So he said,
And made it clear
He wanted action.
A buzz arose:
Rebellion in the air!
He wasn't just ignored,
He had a victory:
On Sunday, the Ward
Served, on special china,
Red sweet peppers
Stuffed with garlic crab.
Worth remarking,
This Conqueror of Drab.
Not often did you see
Such cookery.
Somebody skylarking!
But Amoroso,
Eyes blazing,
In the humming Ward
Lifted up his fist
In triumph
To the Lord!

Recipe For The Bitter Cup

Water poured
In bitterwood cup
Cleans the liver,
Freshens the gut.
Here's the recipe
Old nurses say
Keeps belly sickness
Far away.
Put inside:
Jumby-bead,
Drop of Blood,
Pinewood dust,
If you feel
A little bit
Of coconut peel.
Pass fire near
Three times three
Cool the water
And let it be.
And, remember,
When you drinking
Don't stop
Until you drain
The bitter cup.
When you start
You can't stop
Until you drain
The last gall-drop.

Milkboy

Dazed with sleep, I rise in morning dark.
The call has come: attend a man who's dying,
Old Ramkissoon who no one visited.
His time has come at last to go.
It isn't a big thing, truthfully.
We watched his loneliness so long a time
It's a relief, at least to me:
No one can speak for him I know.
He wanted nothing as I sat nearby.
Except once he asked for water in his cup.
(In all the years he said not one hundred words)
Wet his lips and looked to see my eyes,
Drifted into whispering that was hard to follow.

"Get up, chile, get up, get up!
Time to loose the white cow by the tree.
Bush in flower where bee burn my skin.
Mam so pretty when she vex with me.
Mammy die before my Pappy,
Tears came so bitterly,
Hard Pap try to comfort me,
Hard he try to comfort me.
He gone too, who going mind this baby?
Why he gone so far away?
Why Mammy you gone so far away?
Hear both you calling: chile, get up, get up!
Don't frighten Mammy, don't frighten Pap,
I will mind the white cow in the morning.
Ah, ah, pot so shaky with the spurts of milk."

He sighed and silenced and soon he died.
And I rose soon and went out to hear the morning start.

Benjie Disrobes

Benjie was getting down:
Everyone knew it; he too.
When suddenly one day
He began to take off all his clothes
Everyone thought it must be
Simply his senility.
Not so. Seventy years
In the bosom of the Church
He'd lived and now he knew
Exactly what he had to do.

So far as he was concerned
His time had come.
"Naked into the world
Cometh man
And naked
He goeth out".
He did not feel any more
The need to make a point
Which had been made
A long time gone before.

The Lament Of "Big Bull" Cousins

Tell me the truth!
This could be me?
God loose me in the world
To love women
And women to love me back.
How this could be me!
So maugre and wrinkly-looking,
So mash-up in misery?

Something inside eating me up
Sitting crawly like a slug-king
Taking what it want when
Shrinking up everything.
It like most what most fresh,
Sucking the brain, drawing down the flesh.
It shrivel up the good, thick loins,
It hollow out my jouncy cheeks
Mek big-barrel chest like a little biscuit.
It fattening up fat inside:
Everything else getting trembly and thin.
Years and years it eat and eat
Now it nearly finish and done
Like it want to eat up everything.
It starting East, it going West
Soon it going leave alone by itself
And only the heart in the breast,
Then that eat too and all done!

Skin shine once like silk, man,
Smooth like pure molasses flow
Not a mark on this black man.
Muscle in my belly-pit
Hard as stone, not a fat-ounce:
Knock it, your hand bounce.
Who could mock me,
Match my mastery?

Now look at me good!
This could be me?
Eye never see glass until sixty,
Could sight the old chimney up the coast
From so far like a close-up post:
While people straining, I laughing and reading.
Clear-clear eye, storm-sea grey
Now everything gone and fade away.
Eye full of pink string and boo-boo
Who could play joke so? Who?

Who is it abuse me so?
How who it is could ben' so low?
You could tell why it is,
Why He it is allow this wickedness,
Bitter-bitter after so much sweetness?
I fresh and spright and young,
Next day donkey-drop-dung!
Why life can't fix up a different way?
Why night have to follow bright day?
It could have been organise so
You getting greater as you go:
First is sour, then is spice,
The direction is to Paradise.
So why it couldn't be all we fate
To end up young and bright and straight
From old and scrawny and wither and grey?
It could damn well be fix up that way!

A big, brawly man I was
Big everywhere I tell you,
Big down there too:
Ask any women I know.
Now look how I scrawly!
How this could be so?
There wasn't a woman in town
Didn't know my renown:
Every night
They testing my might.

I teking my pick
When one done, I ready fo' next:
Night have no woman, I vex!
How these days done so quick?

But one woman this heart beat fo' still
I think she dead now forty years.
Sweet, sweet as morning wind
Oh Lord, Lord, she drink like wine!
Eye get heavy with hold-back tears
Watch me now, so dry-up and old
She lucky bad she never get old.
Out of so much she was my One
How quick-and-go that sweet time done.

You could tell me what sense it make
To build something good only fo' break?
I don't understand this big mystery:
A priest-man say it is God decree!
Before I done I going have my say,
Cuss I going cuss, not pray I pray:
I going cuss this God before I die
And He ent have no reason to ask me why.

Request For Softer Spoons

You could get some thicker socks?
Toes turn cold like ice today.

Rice pap, bran, and water-soup:
'A shot of red rum, sweetie doo-doo!"

Cobwebs festoon the dead-dark roof:
Clean and colour it sky-blue.

Door creaking somewhere far away
"Like a funeral parlour hearse."

Raise the bed-head one foot more:
Why, Heaven not near enough for you!

Old man murmuring dirty songs
Disturbed the Ward for one whole week.

Look, she lip paint up so red!
Who she think she is at all?
Matron, what going on in here?
It could be Hotel Belvedere!

Woman only got tears like rain:
Don't let she in here again!
Why all you can't hire bus,
Take we all to a matinee?

Balgobin gone too far this time:
He open the window and take a pee.
What sort of conduct that could be!

So many flies they have in here
We could be carcass-meat one time!

Nurse skirt too, too thin
Or she petticoat didn't put on.
She stand against the sun
Look how brazen panty wearing!

Sweetheart, you know, just thinking this:
Never again I going to get kiss
Until I dead and lay out flat:
Me cold and marble burying.

Gums hurting every time I eat:
You can't get softer spoons in here?

Mammy used to tell me so:
Lonely is a stone pillow.
I miss everything at home so bad:
Why you just can't carry me back?
What medicine when the heart choke up?

Chink-chink frogs too loud at night.
Board got bare-foot splinter wood.

Old this old place old, old, old
They should done and pull it down!
The blasted day, it last too long!
Why are all the plates here round?

Procedure exists to hear each case.
Having to die is a grievance too:
No point registering that complaint,
Though naturally there are some that do.

A Leopard In the Sky

In October
On pure, moonless nights
There is a leopard in the sky.

Above the black outline of trees
Amidst the thousand glittering stars
I trace the daring of its leap.

Night after night
At sea in the terrible boat
He saw the leopard burning in the stars.

Bound from Calcutta
To the sweet green plantations
Gopaul Singh, grown old, remembers only this.

He died here yesterday.
Forever he has made me see
A leopard burn and leap among October stars.

Betty Kumar

In the canteen yesterday at four
Amid the noisy washing up of cups
A simple ceremony a few attended.
The notice set it all out plainly:
"A presentation will be made today
To Betty Kumar well known to all.
Fifty years she served this place:
She goes with Mercy Ward's best wishes".
The new Adminstrator, young and businesslike,
Cracks some jokes and chats to everyone.
No doctors came: none can spare the time.
Matron's there, who knew her as apprentice-nurse.
Cook Stevens from the kitchen came,
The shine of pot-heat on her face,
And Thomas who guards the outside gate:
Old retainers of this ancient place.
A photographer came to take a shot of her.

Tough and stringy Betty Kumar
I look on her in wonder.
Sweet young woman when she started here,
"She had googly eye but silken skin".
And Matron says her back was arrow-straight:
Spine-bone curves now into a humpish shape.
Fifty years she emptied slop-pails in the Ward:
Morning, midday, nine o-clock at night
Cleaned out the urine, spit, and vomit;
Swilling disinfectant, scraped out shit,
Running water sluiced them clean, clean, clean.
The plump young Admin speaks his words of praise
To scattered clapping amid the noisy cups.
"Washroom attendant" is the name he calls,
She hesitates to take his wrapped gold gift:
She does not seem to know what she must do.

Is this a proper way to pass the time on earth?
What Madonna smiles to see this juggling act?
The mind cannot assess a fate like this,
Put value on a lifetime emptying slops.
Fifty years of mornings, noons, and nights
Made brutal habit of Betty Kumar's days:
What can there be that's noble in all this?
I wish I knew much more about her life,
Not only how much shit she moved about.
Did she enjoy the act of love? Did she have children?
What was her home like? What laughter? Dreams?

She puts up her hand in great distress,
The tears come in her googly eyes.
Clutching what she's got, she stumbles slowly back
And then seems loath to leave and go.
She stays as if she fears some doom:
What has she got but tin pails in a stone and scoured room?
Matron takes her by the stringy arms
And leads her to the back door out.
The apprentice-nurses play and nudge and giggle:
Their eyes don't turn a moment as the old ones pass.

Thorn Bush

One day a corn bird, flash of gold,
Got caught in the thorn bush outside.
Something happened: a bird should know bushes.
An old lady saw it from the Ward:
It worried her, she made a great upset.
Brisk nurse Guyadeen went down herself,
Got out the bird and threw it free:
It soared above the mango trees.
The old lady grew pleased, quieted down.
Not such a big event, you'd say.
For some reason I recall that day:
The corn bird fluttering in the thorn;
I was forty and the world seemed old.

God's Work

Mister Edwards, more my good friend
Than gardener and handyman at home,
Served me well for half my life.
Prince, they called him, born about that colonial time:
I called him Mister Edwards until the hour he died.

Strong black face, handsome old man,
Ashy cap of curled short hair,
Never sick a day until a day he sick.
"Wind by the heart", he said
But the heart was sound, too sound,
It took months of agony to kill him
Ripping his guts away slowly
Until that strong, good man was nothing.

"God's work", he would say
When the rain pelted down
And floods rushed in the rivers
And storms lashed the tree-tops.
And "God's work" now he said
When the pain wracked him
Spasms crumpling up his face
Sweat dripping in the effort to hold back
The gut-contracting cry not quite escaping.
"Prince Edwards, he too strong for cry",
But his last day in my arms he cried.
"God's work!"
God should play more.

Calypso

Here is not for emergency
But sometimes there is overflow
And they have to bring them in:
Like this pretty girl in pretty party dress
And tall, young, handsome smashed-up man.
You can tell it's month-end Friday night
Money in his pocket, a girl to court,
After rum and dancing, show-off time:
80 down the avenue by the old train-line,
Life good, the wind sweet.
They're ugly now, butcher's meat.

Try of course, hustle about,
But they're dying, nothing to do;
They're completely out of place too.
They make the Ward restless
Barging in, no patience, such a mess.
Dying has rhythms, fast and slow:
The Ward is waltzing, they calypso.

The Cancer

Strange case.
Rich, debonair, and completely with it
Young Whittaker, the lawyer,
He got cancer and would die.
They made no bones about it,
Opened him and shut him up again,
Told him he had three months, no more.
He took it well, you never know who will:
Straightened all his business with his wife,
Set up a Trust for John Whittaker, his son,
Drank the best malt whisky while he could,
Played the hero part to absolute perfection.
The sun will boil the earth in any case.

Then he seemed to go a little mad:
He checked himself in here, in Mercy Ward.
Understand, this is for the poorest of the poor
And Whittaker was on his way to being very rich.
He came in alone, not even with his wife,
Signed the forms, and settled in his bed:
Visitors who came were most embarrassed.
No plea could budge him; his end came here.
I never found the reason out for sure
(Whoever finds a reason that is sure?)
Turning up the records when he died
I found another Whittaker, named John,
Died in Mercy seven years before.

I puzzled at it, not for long:
Why dig for agonies that are gone?
It lies too near the desperate human heart
To tell for sure how sons and fathers part.

The Fix

You have to get out sometimes,
Take a few days to far away.
The Ward-tension gets too much:
The suffering and lonely pain,
The bursts of unreasonable joy,
The waiting on the waiting on in vain.
A man whispering "No hope, none, none!"
Always on the point of wondering
How lives will end, not how they go on.

The drug of beauty taken pure:
Beloved Essequibo where my soul will go
If hereafter good things happen.
The ballahoo slides in the slow river:
Rose-black water smooth as glass.
Tonight a clear moon lights the land,
The paddle drips silver.
Gold fires in the Mazaruni far away,
Silence and the barking cough of oceolots.
Travel all night and rest at dawn:
Dew glistening on the green banks,
Birds calling before the red comes in the sky
And speeding kingfishers kiss the water.
A bell from somewhere lost in trees
And then a clearing: one man setting nets
And women squeezing white cassava roots.
Waving, we slip through the rose-black water:
They are full of smiles and so are we.
The sun floods over the thick vigorous forest,
Air hums and shines with dragon-flies and rocket-bees,
Between piling clouds and blue sky blazes,
Poui petals, like gold leaves, drift on the river.

These dream-days pass and pall,
My mind drifts back to Mercy Ward:
The ending-up of people in great sadness.
I wake to feel a yearning restlessness:

The itch starts up which needs rough rubbing.
Disturbing things a man must fully face,
A swarm of demons he can't do without.
The gut-attraction of those at risk,
Wounds and danger and utter fear:
Love grows for it when you are safely near.
There's intensity in living through
A dying that's not your own.
There's always power in the air,
Shine of courage flicking off and on.
The hard habits and the daily dealing
With mortal crises in the Ward
Gives life a pitch and rigorous meaning
From which, I think, there is no weaning.
Why do you think that wars go on?
No mild or sacred wand can catch
The lightning from the sky or match
The fascination of the sword.
After beauty's gentle fix, I need
The sharper fix of Mercy Ward.

Mother Tango

There is always some cruelty in nick-names.
They called her Mother Tango in the street
Not because she, being young and strong,
Became some legend on the dancing floor.
She got her name, and no one knows another,
Since she was very small and fell
And never was the same again:
A hip dis-jointed and a stunted leg
Made of her walk a comic twist and dip.

It must be bitter to be laughed at all your life.
There never was a sign of bitterness in her,
Nor is there now that anyone can see.
She smiled at all and never was affronted.
She lived a frugal life, she served her Church:
In place of those she never had, or could,
She mothered orphans fifty years and more.

Her life ends here, she will never go back out.
In part-thanks for her love and work she's done
A young Jesuit comes to visit her:
He holds her hand and gives Communion bread.
The young priest looks disturbed: he's sad:
Perhaps he hears the jeers of "Mother Tango!" still
He should not be sad: when all is said and done.
She can sideways drag herself to Heaven
Faster than you or I can ever walk or run.

Bird-song

Sky, colour of agouti, drips rain,
A strong wind blows in the gulls from the sea.
Young boy in a blue jacket, head hunched,
Bicycles in carrying a pan of milk.

Every morning he comes without fail.
The pan clanks against the bike's side:
It's for his grandmother in Mercy Ward.
The sound wakens me like bird-song.

Last Breath: Still Life With Fan

Silence from the sea;
The still night
Holds its breath.
In the lamp-light
Her living face
Carved by shadows
Looks not very different
From what is soon to be
Her decomposing face.
She has left uneaten
Rose-fleshed pomegranates,
Bread, and chick-pea brew.
Pearls of pale sweet
Bead her high brow.
It is a stifling hour:
The few deep breaths she takes
Seem precious things to do.

On the brown, iron bedside table
She's dropped an old fan delicate as fern.
Ivory stems pinned with silver pins:
Torn yellow silk opening in between
Shows red plums on a tree with birds.
Lace gone black tatters on the spray of bone.
Sweetheart's gift now nearly all used up,
It lies abandoned, heirloom at its end.
Framed beyond all further composition
She'll never pick it up again it seems.
Glossy grape-skin once, now so raisin-withered,
Blue-veined, liver-freckled hand
Plucks weakly at the congealed sheet.
A nurse in passing senses what is wanted:
An ancient grace is reasserted.
How honourable are simple, well-learned ways!
A practised gesture with a lovely thing
At once transforms the gesturer:

What gathered round this death's defeated,
What is brutal falls away,
Momentarily all's not lost.
Life's pattern knits up anew:
What's to come has been before,
What has gone may re-appear.
All's not settled, all's unsure:
The picture can be drawn again.
If only briefly, she fans the breathless air.

Love Affair

At four precisely every afternoon,
She starts preparing for the visitor.
She smooths the sheets and tidies up all round:
Her house to keep has narrowed down to this.
She dresses carefully and puts sweet talcum on,
Grey hair she combs as much as can be combed,
And settles in her chair, folds her hands and waits.
Her day, her life, concentrated in this hour:
Her eyes intently turn towards the opened door.

At five precisely every afternoon
He comes in through the door at visiting hour.
His suit is shiny-old but pressed and clean.
He takes off an old beret on entering the Ward,
He leans quite heavily upon a worn-wood cane.
Without fail he shyly gives a wave towards her bed,
Then slowly stumps towards her and she looks content.

Quietly they sit together near the tidy bed:
They hardly speak a word the whole hour he is here.
She bends a little closer, he gives a half-way smile.
She rocks a while and he relaxes.
But there is something in the closeness of the chairs:
Strangers would be further, even friends not half so near.
They doubly occupy a single space in time:
That space is empty if he for one's not there.

At five to six he rises from his usual place.
She looks at him, he gives her half a nod
And bends stiffly down and touches her old cheek
And takes her hand in his and she takes his:
No words exchanged, and that is all there is.
At exactly six o'clock, when visiting hour ends,
He goes towards the door and does not turn at all.
Her sadness deeper than our customary sorrow,
She turns away and yearns towards tomorrow.

The Place They Have To Go

When someone checks into Mercy Ward
One of the particulars you have to get
Is what provision has been made
For a burial costing nothing, net.
They look restless and turn away.
Even if you have a few days only
You don't want to think of the black hearse
Pulled by the half-blind City horses
Or about Merriman's fourth best limousine
Rattling unattended through the streets.
And you don't want to know
About that part of the graveyard
Where no flowers grow, just tussocky grass
And nettles and black-ant nests.

You often have to visit where they go:
A bare field where goats are grazed,
Rust-coloured grasshoppers whirring as you step.
Across the way the splendid tombs arise
White and shaded by huge impressive trees:
Marble blossoms deck them down the years.
And ornaments and wreaths in perfect alabaster.
But here of course no momuments arise:
Graves dug in line straight into earth.
When freshly dug slap-dash dirt-mounds show
With wooden crosses stuck awry on top:
Rain crumbles them shapeless in a month or so.
This field of grass and goat-weed
Holds a bare and hopeless dignity.

The Supervisor's office is a simple place:
A chair, a desk, a concrete vault
Where archives of all burials are kept;
The leather-covered volumes stretch centuries back.
It sets things in persepctive right away:
The record is equal in these careful books,
Inscribes for all an austere common fate.

No space for high or space for low:
The line of written detail does not change,
All are put down here the same,
Bare, unblemished soul-mates, row on row.
In the field you do not get to see
The part of burial that does not show
Obscurity or utmost fame:
The scene below is much the same.

Hawk-wing or Stone

Walk around outside the Ward
There's so much bustle about nothing.
The streets busy with what?
Some sort of treadmill:
People passing and re-passing.
The having to eat and to plan eating.
The purchasing and delivering.
Where's the edge on anything?

Back here, deep in each one
Life or death's the thing:
Even that's minor in the end.
No more lies.
Nothing, everything?
Clean down to bone:
Will I rise
Or fall
Like hawk-wing
Or stone?

Runtee

"Runtee" Tang-Choon, yellow as a Lima bean,
Was brought in like a bundle by the police:
"Little grasshopper, he light as leaf', they said.
They found him in the cold morning crumpled up,
Old clothes tied with string, small torn black boots,
By Alonzo's rum shop in Anira Street:
He could have been dumped out of a rubbish bin.
The nurses roughly rubbed his skin, roughly wrapped him up
To make him last a little while at least;
Matron brought him dumpling soup he would not take.
Black eyes dying, he never said a word.
He had a sort of pride not easy to describe:
A fearlessness when fear has ceased to count.

Scuttling little four-foot huckster man
(Calf-muscles hard as iron even at the end)
Sold roasted peanuts around the town for years
Moved so fast from crowded street to street
The children called him "Mile-a-Minute" man.
His whole life spent in carrying nuts and walking,
Savage sun or pelting rain was all the same,
He never seemed to stop for long enough to sell.
The worst among the urchins robbed him once a week,
Set him asprawl and laughed as he got up:
"Mile-a-Minute on the road again!"
He'd look away, hoist his sack, hustle on his way.
He seemed to have no friends or anyone at all
And nobody ever knew what hole he had to go.

Chinamen don't end up here: they mind their own.
None ever came for "Runtee" Tang-Choon though.
Five days here he lasted, never said a word.
Black eyes like shining beads, hardly winking,
Trapped animal, except he never trembled once.
Small as a child, his chest sunk in
He frightened me more than anyone I know.
Something about him far beyond forlorn:
This little man should never have been born!

I cannot think that: no man's life is waste.
No one stopped in kindness or gave him half a thought.
A life and death so lonely teaches best:
"All that lives needs help from all the rest".

Blue Potaro Hills

Old Oudit Ram seemed, to those who knew,
To have taken up permanent residence
In the coveted corner bed on the Western side.
He had even accumulated a few belongings,
A litter of small items to grace his stay,
A sort of shrine to give a sort of meaning
To his sort of life: a holy Hindu picture, a tattered book,
A bag of stones (I don't know why), a faded Panam bag.
He seemed to have settled in for good, or bad,
And he behaved himself and said his prayers and ate.

Without any warning, at evening time one day,
He suprised the Ward by getting up and walking out.
He showed every sign of knowing what he did,
Collecting up his picture, book, and rocks,
And also his small bag, and making for the door.
He got quite far, almost to the stairs outside
Before the shouts brought order back again,
And he was hustled back to stay in bed
Where he belonged, the nurses told him scoldingly,
And not where he was trying hard to go,
As he explained: home, home, one time more,
Home, far away and far to go,
Home where he remembered in the evening mist
Blue Potaro hills of young days long ago.

WITHDRAWN
SCOTTISH POETRY LIBRARY
Court 14 High Street
Edinburgh EH1 1TE
Tel: 031-557 2876